Interviewing Engineering Graduates

Hire the best in engineering talent

Connor Skye Riley

Impackt Publishing
We Mean Business

Interviewing Engineering Graduates

First published: October 2014

Production reference: 1101014

Published by Impackt Publishing Ltd.
Livery Place
35 Livery Street
Birmingham B3 2PB, UK.

ISBN 978-1-78300-010-4

www.Impacktpub.com

Credits

Author

Connor Skye Riley

Reviewer

Nataliya Zub

Commissioning Editor

Danielle Rosen

Copy Editors

Simran Bhogal

Ameesha Green

Faisal Siddiqui

Project Coordinators

Anurag Banerjee

Venitha Cutinho

Proofreaders

Maria Gould

Ameesha Green

Paul Hindle

Production Coordinator

Melwyn D'sa

Cover Work

Simon Cardew

About the Author

Connor Skye Riley is a software engineer specializing in user experience design and frontend web development. She has experience both in conducting technical interviews and in working closely with technical recruiters to develop software products.

In teaching web development courses, she has counseled students on what to expect from their first technical interviews. With nearly a decade of professional experience at companies ranging from some of the largest in the world to scrappy startups, she has spent considerable time thinking about how and why we recruit engineers the way we do.

About the Reviewer

Nataliya Zub has been part of the IT industry since 2003. Currently, she serves as the head of HR and recruitment for an American business technology outsourcing company called Innovecs, with responsibility for leading the strategy of the department, ensuring follow-through HR best practices, and accelerating global growth initiatives.

Innovecs was built from the ground up on a highly competitive market. For 2 years, Innovecs managed to start more than 15 cutting-edge projects requiring nonstandard engineering solutions, and hired more than 200 top-level engineers.

Prior to joining Innovecs, Nataliya had served as a Human Resources Consultant for a number of international outsourcing companies, IT start-up projects, and new market entries looking to set up business in Ukraine.

She brings hands-on experience in building and developing successful engineering teams for new market entries and start-up projects within fast-growing, high-tech organizations.

Nataliya earned her Master's degree in Computer Science from the National University of Ukraine, Kiev Polytechnic Institute, and Bachelor's degree in Psychology from the National Pedagogical University.

Contents

Preface

The hiring market for engineers is rapidly expanding. Technologists and engineers are increasingly in demand to fill jobs as companies try to automate their processes and do business in an increasingly technology-driven world. In a market where demand for talent is high, recruiters and managers are under a lot of pressure to hire new team members in a quick and efficient way.

However, the process of hiring an employee who commands an engineer's high salary is very complex. Scarcity of talent means that regular methods of advertising open jobs don't get you as many good candidates. Often, hiring managers lament that candidates who are brought in for interviews lack basic technical skills. The process of interviewing a new engineer gets more and more complicated and expensive as business needs grow more complex.

Engineering candidates looking for a new job face concerns as well. There may be dozens of fitting job descriptions available, but most read like uninspiring laundry lists of skills the candidate must have. Companies expect candidates to go through days of interviews without ever meeting their prospective teammates or learning what problems they'll be working on. Even after spending days on interviews, some companies simply never contact the candidate again, leaving them with a fairly low opinion of that company.

This book presents a simple step-by-step guide you help you avoid these pitfalls and successfully navigate the complex process of hiring engineers. With actionable advice, tips, and examples, you will have more engineering candidates to choose from and be more confident that those you hire are the best of the best.

The goal of this book is to help you consider each step in your existing hiring process from the specific perspective of hiring an engineer. Rather than a comprehensive guide to hiring in general, this book presents examples, outlines, and guides to the parts of the process you can specifically tailor to attract new technical talent. Filling a job is a marketing opportunity, and engineering candidates are your customers.

What this book covers

Chapter 1, The Job Description, covers the best way to market your company to engineering applicants. This includes how to communicate the responsibilities of the position to best appeal to a technical applicant, how to encourage applicants who fit your company's culture, and how to ensure that the technical requirements of the job are clear and precise.

Chapter 2, Recruiting Engineers, provides novel ideas for networking with engineers and building your corporate brand within the engineering community.

Chapter 3, The Phone Screening, includes a guide for HR representatives to evaluate the most important nontechnical qualities of an engineer, including sample questions.

Chapter 4, Code Tests, discusses what kinds of tests are most effective, how to write them, and how to evaluate candidates' work.

Chapter 5, In-person Interviews, provides checklists and guides to ensure that every person involved in the interview is prepared to best represent the company and evaluate the interviewee.

Chapter 6, Follow-up, Negotiation, and Closing a Hire, outlines a process for managing post-interview communication between all the parties involved; this is especially important in interviewing technical talent because of the expense and manpower necessary to evaluate candidates.

Who this book is for

This book is for you if you have ever:

> ➤ Struggled to write an engineering job description
> ➤ Been disappointed in the quality of applicants you get from online job advertisements
> ➤ Felt that your screening process was not getting you very good interview candidates
> ➤ Felt disorganized or unprepared when interviewing an engineering candidate
> ➤ Saw that good candidates slipped through the cracks during any phase of the hiring process

For HR representatives who are active in the hiring process but are not engineers, this book will give you an insight into how to make your company's jobs stand out and get engineers excited about working for you. For technical managers, this book will help you streamline your hiring processes so that you select better candidates earlier in the process and spend less time and money interviewing candidates who are a poor fit.

No matter what your role is, this book will provide you with easy-to-follow steps to the process of finding, interviewing, and hiring engineers. Using these guides and examples, you and your company will be able to build a stronger and more cohesive technical team.

Conventions

In this book, you will find a number of styles of text that distinguish between different kinds of information. Here are some examples of these styles, and an explanation of their meaning.

New terms and **important words** are shown in bold.

Make a note

Warnings or important notes appear in a box like this.

Tip

Tips and tricks appear like this.

List

List appear like this

Action Point

Action points appear like this

Reader feedback

Feedback from our readers is always welcome. Let us know what you think about this book—what you liked or may have disliked. Reader feedback is important for us to develop titles that you really get the most out of.

To send us general feedback, simply send an e-mail to feedback@impacktpub.com, and mention the book title via the subject of your message.

Piracy

Piracy of copyright material on the Internet is an ongoing problem across all media. At Packt, we take the protection of our copyright and licenses very seriously. If you come across any illegal copies of our works, in any form, on the Internet, please provide us with the location address or website name immediately so that we can pursue a remedy.

Please contact us at copyright@impacktpub.com with a link to the suspected pirated material.

We appreciate your help in protecting our authors, and our ability to bring you valuable content.

>1

The Job Description

There's a lot of competition for top engineering talent out there. Companies are increasingly eager to hire new talent from a relatively small pool of candidates. It's tough to get noticed when your company's jobs are up against so many others. So how do you make your open positions stand out? The key is to think about your job descriptions as actual advertisements designed to get engineers excited about working for your company!

In this chapter, we'll cover:

> ➤ A simple framework that will vastly improve every job description you write

> ➤ What to emphasize to get engineers interested

> ➤ How to avoid common mistakes when writing engineering job descriptions

> ➤ How and where to promote your vacancy

A universal job description framework

Before you start writing, it's important to understand what separates an ordinary job description from an outstanding one. A great job description:

> ➤ **Keeps it short**: There's no need to get bogged down in details. Use the space you have to sell prospective candidates the unique problems your company solves.

> ➤ **Builds on success**: Do your research and read other job descriptions for positions like yours. How are top companies in your industry writing their job openings? How can you do it better?

> ➤ **Sells your company culture**: Personality counts! Be clear about what kind of team member succeeds at your company and you'll attract like-minded people.

> ➤ **Gets candidates excited**: Always ask yourself, "Why should this candidate want to work for my company?", and craft every sentence to answer that question.

Just like every building begins with a solid foundation, every job description should follow from a solid framework. Think of the following sections as a checklist or guide to organizing your thoughts as you write.

Start with a concise title

Job titles should clearly indicate the level of the position (for example, Entry Level, Expert, or Lead) and the role in just a few words. Research what other companies in your industry call a given position to make sure your titles are similar.

Tip

Browsing versus searching for job titles

Most jobs are posted online, and the job title can make or break the visibility of the job description. If the job is going to be posted on a small job board, you may consider treating the job title as more of a catchy headline. For example:

"Raise your hand if you want to build iPad apps!"

"Seeking UI Engineer with great design sense"

If people are going to be searching for your job, keep the title short, standard, and clear. For example:

- ▪ "Lead Medical Device Engineer"
- ▪ "Environmental Engineer, Wastewater Treatment"

About your company

This should be where you answer, "Why should I want to work for your company?" in a few sentences. This section should definitely not look like standard company boilerplate! Every position calls for a slightly different description of the work environment; remember that you're advertising to a distinct group of candidates. Depending on the position, you might mention the following points:

> ➤ Company description, including recent milestones and growth

> ➤ Office environment and employee perks

> ➤ Team size and structure

> ➤ Employee benefits package

Who you're looking for

Use this section to help candidates see themselves in this position. Be clear about the duties this person must perform, but keep in mind the kind of social and cultural fit you're looking for too. In general, try to cover the following:

> ➤ Why this position is open

> ➤ Technical details of the project you're hiring for

> ➤ Qualities of the ideal candidate

> ➤ Expected responsibilities for this position

> ➤ Hours, travel requirements, contract details, or salary expectations

Requirements

Ideally, the technical requirements should be one of the shortest and quickest sections of any job description you write. Don't throw in everything but the kitchen sink. The following is all you really need:

> ➤ Three to four bare minimum requirements

> ➤ A ranked list of no more than ten nice-to-have requirements

With the preceding outline, you'll be able to start writing tighter, more effective job descriptions for any type of position. The following sections will take a more focused look at how to tailor your job descriptions to engineering positions.

What engineers look for in a job description

This section will take a more focused look at how to tailor your job descriptions to engineering positions. When you emphasize the right features of your company and job, you'll attract more engineers who are passionate about solving problems and building great products. So, what gets top candidates interested?

A clear picture of what you're building

Engineering candidates want to build products they can get excited about. The opportunity to tell all of our friends that we helped build an exciting product is a major reward of being an engineer. So, take the opportunity to show off what your company is building in the job description!

If your company is hiring engineers to work on a new or early-stage product that you haven't publicized yet, it's easy to be too coy and speak in general terms. There are reasons to not share too much information, of course. But which of the following jobs sound more interesting?

> ➤ "Stealth startup seeks data analysis wizard to help us shake up social media."

> ➤ "We're a small team building a platform to connect independent contractors and homeowners in a trustworthy, transparent marketplace. We're looking for a passionate self-starter to help us scale our product to reach a national audience."

The first job description is obviously more generic. "Social media" is a very saturated market, and the description provides no detail about what the company proposes to do differently. The second one is better; simply, it provides concrete details about what is being built and for whom.

I encourage you to be as specific as possible about what you're actually hiring someone to make. No candidate wants to come into an interview with no idea about the product they'll be working on!

Interesting problems to solve

A surprisingly large amount of the day-to-day routine of being an engineer is figuring out if what you're building has already been built, and repurposing existing solutions to fit your current needs. While an engineer who does this well will save huge amounts of time and money, they will never find it as exciting as solving a problem that nobody else has ever solved.

Survey your engineering team members about the last project they had that got them excited. If you want to attract technological innovators, advertise how your team is already inventing new solutions.

Your engineering team's culture

Tell potential applicants a little about what the culture of your engineering team is like. Are engineers encouraged to work with other departments? Does your office layout support collaboration or individual privacy? Be sure to mention whether your engineers work with other teams at other locations, and whether working from home is encouraged or discouraged at your company.

Does your organization have codified company values? How do these relate to the engineering team? Do you encourage engineers to give back to the community? To pursue side projects? To manage their own time?

Additionally, if the position presents a great opportunity for personal growth, continuing education, mentorship, or leadership opportunities, be sure to mention that in the job description.

A clear idea of who you're looking for

Ideally, every engineering candidate would be a highly domain-experienced, efficient, seasoned professional. Realistically, these are tough to find. Be realistic about what role you need filled—does this person absolutely need to be an expert in order to do the job? Would a generalist who learns quickly and works well in a small team be a better fit? Give an accurate picture of who you imagine the ideal candidate to be and the applicants you get will be those who can see themselves in that role.

Day-to-day expectations

If you can, it's good to give engineering candidates an idea of the day-to-day process your engineering team follows (for example, mention if the team follows scrum or other agile development processes). Every company, team, and individual does their best work under different conditions, and you will have more success in hiring if your applicants know that their work style fits your engineering team's style.

What does your typical product lifecycle or release schedule look like? Some engineers thrive in an environment where new code is released every day, while others want to work on projects that are perfected over the course of months and then delivered.

Does the team follow any particular engineering methodology? How are engineers expected to participate in product development and planning? Many of these questions boil down to how much of the engineer's time will be spent in meetings. Every candidate will have a different idea of what works for him or her.

A note on buzzwords

What's wrong with the following job description?

> *"Rockstar Software Developer wanted: Must have a killer portfolio and open source project experience. Are you a code ninja with a take-no-prisoners attitude? Then we want to hire you!"*

"Rockstar", "ninja", "killer", "take-no-prisoners"... kind of violent, isn't it? This is a contrived example, but there's a definite trend amongst smaller companies and up-and-coming startups to overuse buzzwords like these to communicate a sense that they have a fun, youthful, or innovative culture and are looking for fitting candidates.

Do you really want to hire a destructive, self-centered rockstar? A ninja who operates outside of the team? Probably not! It's best to clearly communicate what you actually want in an employee rather than relying on buzzwords to hopefully do it for you.

Don't prematurely limit your candidate pool—be clear about who you're looking for without using buzzwords.

Writing technical job requirements

Writing technical job requirements can be daunting, especially if you're not personally familiar with the technologies the engineers in your organization use. I encourage you to get input early on from the engineers who will be working with a new hire to get a sense of what the requirements should be.

Keep the list of absolute must-have requirements to three or four bullet points. Talk to your engineering team members to understand what skills are necessary on day one to do the job, and leave everything else as nice-to-have. Each extra must-have decreases the number of qualified applicants you'll get and increases the amount of time it will take to find a good hire.

Phrase technical requirements in terms of results rather than specific tools where possible. Requirements like "Experience developing rich interactive web applications" or "Proficiency with CAD software to design complex mechanical components" leaves room for candidates who may not know the specific tools your engineers use, but can demonstrate that they have achieved the level of results your organization needs.

Ask candidates to prove their skills rather than just match the keywords in your job description. Require candidates to show an online portfolio, code samples, or other meaningful work deliverables that demonstrate past accomplishments. This is an excellent must-have requirement because it gives candidates the opportunity to show off their skills, but doesn't constrain them to one technology.

Getting the word out

Using the previous tips, you've written an exciting, unique job description for your open engineering position. After you've posted your job to your company website, along with your large job boards of choice, what more can you do?

There are many online communities which run tech-focused job boards; these will put your job description in front of the right audience.

Make a note

Look for communities which provide resources for engineers, like Stack Overflow (`careers.stackoverflow.com`), professional organizations like the Society of Women Engineers (`careers.swe.org`), or tech news communities like TechCrunch (`crunchboard.com`).

Make sure you get a feel for the individual community before posting; smaller communities might respond better to a more casual writing style, for instance.

With persistence and careful targeting of your job advertisements, you will quickly see a benefit in the quantity and quality of applicants your job descriptions draw in.

Summary

In this chapter, we have learned how to:

➤ Use a universal framework to write tighter, more effective job descriptions

➤ Get engineers interested by understanding what they look for in a job description

➤ Avoid buzzwords

➤ Write better technical job requirements

➤ Promote the job description in all the right places

Next, we will discuss how to go beyond job postings and start actively recruiting engineers.

>2

Recruiting Engineers

If you've tried to fill open engineering positions in the past, you know it isn't enough to simply post a job description, no matter how well written and well placed it may be. Highly skilled positions may get very few applicants no matter what you do. You can be proactive in searching for and reaching out to ideal applicants, but how can you best pique their interest?

With engineers especially, it's additionally important to always be contacting new candidate leads. Even if your company has no open positions, a valuable recruit is almost always a welcome addition to the team. This chapter will give you the tools you need to reach out to engineers to ensure you always have a pool of potential candidates.

In this chapter, we'll cover:

➤ How to improve your response rate when you reach out to recruits

➤ How to maximize your employee referral potential

➤ What to look for in engineers' resumes

➤ How to look beyond a candidate's resume to identify top talent

Online recruiting

Online search engines and recruiting tools can help you find many qualified candidates with ease, but what they can't guarantee is any candidate you reach out to ever contacting you back. When you're reaching out to a potential hire, especially for high-value engineering positions, you need to communicate in a compelling way to give you an edge over the competition.

Pitfalls to avoid

Social media and other online tools have made it easy for recruiters to search for and discover engineers whose work experience closely fits their job openings. Unfortunately, it also means that nearly every engineer I know has a fairly low view of recruitment e-mails. Usually this is annoyance at the behavior of third-party recruiters. Common complaints include:

> ➤ **Not knowing when to quit, using the wrong channels, and ignoring a poor fit**: It is in recruiter's interests to cast as wide a net for talent as possible; it costs very little to e-mail lots of people about an opportunity, even if few of them are at all qualified. This means that engineers end up with inboxes full of uninteresting recruitment e-mails. In the same way, recruiters have no reason not to keep e-mailing the same candidates even if they have never received a response. When this behavior expands to unsolicited phone calls it can become very invasive.

> ➤ **Refusing to give details**: As a recruiter's success is based on successfully brokering the process of providing candidates to companies, they often leave out a lot of the details that get engineers excited about positions. This is mostly to prevent candidates going directly to the employer.

If your company uses third-party recruiters to help fill positions, rest assured that effective technical recruiters will avoid the worst of this behavior. If you're interested in getting a better response when you personally reach out to candidates, read on.

Improving your response rate

When you e-mail potential recruits, keep the following points in mind. These tips will help your messages stand out from the flood of recruitment emails:

> ➤ **Be personal**: You chose to reach out to this particular candidate for a reason; help them see clearly what it is about their experience that you think makes them qualified. Tell the candidate how their interests and your company's interests are similar. Have a look at the following examples:

> ➤ **Bad**: "It seems like many of your projects and skills would be a good fit for what we're doing."

> ➤ **Good**: "I see that you've contributed to various libraries for supporting website internationalization; we're ramping up our localization efforts for our global release and have some unique challenges in this area that might interest you."

➤ **Demonstrate value**: If you can find out anything about a potential recruit's interests, values, or personality, then you have a great opportunity to tell them how your company can support them. At least make the perks of working for your company clear, but putting a personal spin on things is always welcome. Have a look at the following examples:

> ➤ "I noticed that you've volunteered as a technical resource for Habitat for Humanity; we encourage our engineers to take one day a week to work on side projects like this. As a company, we also organize yearly giving to nonprofit organizations our employees care about."

> ➤ "Our hiring manager was very impressed with your blog posts on organizing remote engineering teams; we offer flex time for employees who wish to work from home and would be very interested in your suggestions for optimizing remote employee contributions."

➤ **Get hiring managers to reach out**: If you're a hiring manager, or you can get upper management involved in reaching out to candidates, definitely do so. For instance, a short phone call from a hiring manager is a quick way to give candidates direct insight into the project they are being hired for. An email from a VP of Technology or another manager is both flattering to a potential candidate and indicates that someone at the company really understands how their experience is directly applicable to the company's efforts.

Networking

Most professionals understand the importance of networking for their individual careers. This section will show you how your engineering team can actually network on behalf of your company to benefit your hiring organization.

Employee referrals

Any recruiting professional will tell you that employee referrals are an invaluable source of new talent for any organization. While referrals may make up only a small part of the resumes you consider for a position, the candidates are usually remarkably well suited for that position and your company, since an employee who understands your company has preselected that candidate for you.

If your company doesn't have one, I encourage you to develop an official Employee Referral Program, so that everyone in the company is aware of your referral policies and employee referrals are handled in a regular way. Even a few referred candidates can make a huge difference to your ability to fill positions quickly. Use the following tips to maximize your engineering referrals:

> **Encourage your engineers to pursue passion projects**: A passion project is simply a project that an employee pursues either inside or outside of work just for the fun of making something. They're also one of the best possible ways for engineers to network with other engineers. Passion projects give engineers the opportunity to build on the work of their peers, which often involves seeking advice, help, or collaboration with engineers who don't work for your company. Encourage engineers to make these contacts, as one of them may be the perfect fit for an open position in the future.

> **Make referrals easy**: Notify your engineers when new job openings arise and when they are filled. Make regular e-mail updates on open positions a part of your Employee Referral Program. Adding social media sharing options to your online job postings will make it easy for employees to get the word out to their contacts.

> **Incentivize properly**: More and more companies are offering large monetary rewards to employees who refer key hires. It's not appropriate for every company, but in many geographic markets, it's smart for companies to offer up to several thousand dollars for a referred engineering hire. Any meaningful monetary incentive should be presented as a way to recognize a referring employee's valuable contribution to the company.

Tip

Employees are unlikely to take unfair advantage of referral bonuses, but you can explicitly discourage submitting too many referral resumes for one position. Additionally, try to avoid the impression of unfairness by excluding upper management from your referral bonus program.

> **Follow up**: Treat referred candidates like the valuable leads they are and follow up with them quickly after they cross your desk. Don't let the trail go cold; it's likely to discourage the candidate and the employee who referred him or her. And definitely don't forget to give your employees feedback. If a resume wasn't a good fit, let them know why. If a candidate was a great fit, don't forget to say thank you!

Become part of the community

Most cities, small and large, have an active community of science, technology, and engineering professionals. For companies in major metropolitan areas, chances are that there are already organizations that dedicate themselves to hosting networking events, friendly competitions, or professional talks aimed at engineers. Offering your office space to host such an event is a great way to get your employees talking to outside engineers without having to manage the event yourself.

Get your employees involved in planning events they want to attend. Company happy hour can quickly expand into community happy hour. Engineering employees may want to start weekly lectures, tutorials, or intra-office competitions. All of these are great opportunities for your employees to learn something new, and if successful, can be opened up to the professional public.

Tip

Don't treat networking events like explicit recruiting opportunities. You wouldn't want to make guests feel like they've been fooled into a sales pitch for your company. Think of events as building your company's social capital and brand among the engineering community. They're a great perk for employees, too.

Evaluating candidates

With well-written job descriptions and creative strategies for actively recruiting candidates, you will soon find yourself with a pile of resumes to evaluate. You don't have unlimited time to read each one, so it's important to decide in advance what qualities you're looking for. You likely already have a set of basic qualifiers in mind (minimum GPA, lack of spelling errors, and so on); this section will help you identify the very best candidates amongst resumes that meet your basic requirements.

Reading resumes

Remember that a resume doesn't represent a candidate's engineering skills; it represents their communication skills. It's very important that an engineering candidate is able to effectively communicate their technical accomplishments and tell you about projects they've worked on. The following are some of the most important indicators of an outstanding resume:

> ➤ **Language tailored to the job description**: A good candidate knows that you only have a short time to read their resume, and phrases their accomplishments so that you see their experience reflected through the lens of your job description. This means organizing their resume so that relevant experience is emphasized and echoes key words and phrases from your job description when applicable.

> ➤ **Result-oriented, represents accomplishments well**: It's important that an engineering candidate is able to communicate what was actually accomplished by their work. Great candidates will identify what they personally accomplished, rather than phrasing their contribution as part of a team effort. Have a look at the following examples:
>
>> ➤ **Poor**: "Supported datacenter and web infrastructure team."
>>
>> ➤ **Good**: "Worked with usability specialists to develop a web-based prototype of new installation and licensing system."
>>
>> ➤ **Great**: "Optimized existing part schematics for manufacturing, saving $30,000 in annual materials costs."

> ➤ **Demonstrates an understanding of personal strengths**: Most candidates will list their skills and the tools they are familiar with. Great candidates will interpret these skills in a way that helps you understand what they are good at. Look for candidates who have a well-written objective section or clearly communicate what value they will bring to your company. Have a look at the following examples:
>
>> ➤ **Okay**: "Skills: CSS, HTML, Javascript, jQuery."
>>
>> ➤ **Good**: "Skills: Expert understanding of Javascript, 4 years' experience."
>>
>> ➤ **Great**: "Core competencies: Developed rich user interfaces in JavaScript, CSS, and HTML by integrating feedback from end users and analytics data."

Tip

A note on software engineers: I have known too many great software engineers who started out as scientists, mathematicians, or artists, so it's important to understand that education isn't everything on an engineer's resume. Certainly attending a top school and earning a high GPA are strong indicators of a good candidate, but an unusual educational background would cause me to look closely at the projects a candidate has worked on rather than rejecting that candidate outright.

Looking beyond the resume

It's an unfortunate truth that some candidates with strong resumes and impressive descriptions of their experience come into interviews and turn out not to be competent in the right technologies. You can reduce these false positives early in the process by looking for candidates who back up their clearly worded resume with proof of their accomplishments. The following are a few things to look for:

> ➤ **Personal blogs or online writing**: It's fairly standard for engineering candidates to have a professional website and to list it on their resume. Read what candidates have written on their website; some of the best candidates will be passionate enough about what they do to share their inventions, technical issues, and discoveries with the world.

➤ **Code samples or other project contributions**: Just like professional artists should have portfolios, good engineering candidates should be sharing samples of their work on their personal websites. Even new graduates should be displaying the results of their coursework or thesis projects. If you're looking for someone to write code, candidates who have a public GitHub account or noted contributions to open source projects give you or the hiring manager yet another way to accurately evaluate their technical skills.

Summary

In this chapter, you learned how to:

➤ Reach out to engineers in a way that stands out and avoids common annoyances

➤ Encourage your employees to refer engineering candidates

➤ Build your company brand and make contacts by providing value to the engineering community

➤ Identify excellent communication skills on engineers' resumes

➤ Evaluate an engineer's technical skills using online portfolios and work samples

In the next chapter, we'll look at the first step in narrowing down your pool of candidates: the phone screening.

≫3

The Phone Screening

After you have narrowed down your pool of candidates to the strongest resumes, phone interviews are a standard next step within which to formally introduce your company to a candidate. They are a quick, inexpensive way to gauge a candidate's interest in your company and confirm the skills and experience on their resume.

In this chapter, we will learn:

> ➤ Which goals to keep in mind during the phone screening
> ➤ How to evaluate a candidates' non-technical skills
> ➤ How to ask good technical questions
> ➤ What questions to expect from top candidates

Organizing the phone screening

Part of the reason why a phone screening is such a good evaluation tool is that it only requires you and the candidate to set aside 30 minutes to an hour to speak. Time investment and scheduling difficulties are minimal.

Contact the candidate well in advance to set up a time to speak. Many candidates will prefer to use Skype or Google Hangouts to conduct phone screening, depending on their schedule. Be flexible and understand that some candidates will be scheduling interviews around their normal workday responsibilities.

For an engineering candidate, you ought to be covering fairly technical concepts during the interview. If you are an HR representative and don't have technical expertise, you'll likely be asking questions on behalf of a more technical manager, which may be difficult. If it's possible for your company, you might split the phone screen into a non-technical phone screen, which you conduct, and a technical screen, which engineering employees conduct, if you're more comfortable that way.

Overall, there are just a few questions you should keep in mind while screening a candidate:

> ➤ Could I work with this person? Does their personality fit in with our team?
> ➤ Does this candidate tell a story about his or her experience that matches and builds upon what's on his or her resume?
> ➤ Can this candidate talk intelligently about basic technical concepts that they should understand based on their resume?
> ➤ Can this candidate think creatively about solving engineering problems?
> ➤ What is this candidate's motivation for changing positions?
> ➤ Is this candidate excited about working for my company?

Your goal during a phone screening should be to answer all of these questions with confidence.

Introducing your company

As you begin the phone screening, remember that it is yet another opportunity for you to sell the experience of working at your company. Spend a few minutes reviewing your company and products for the candidate, as well as covering what the role entails and the sorts of problems the candidate can expect to work on if hired. You might also mention the structure of the engineering team, and the office environment in general. You have a few minutes, so feel free to go into greater detail than in the job description.

Treat the introduction like a conversation, not a lecture. A good candidate will participate and ask questions, understanding that the next part of the interview will likely involve introducing him or herself to you. Your goal should be to introduce the role in enough detail so that the candidate understands why you are asking them the questions that follow.

The introduction also helps you get the ball rolling so that you can guide the conversation. Overall, in a phone screening, you shouldn't feel that the candidate is doing all the talking. You should always be asking clarifying questions, keeping your goals in mind, and directing the flow of the conversation. You are driving the interview, not the candidate.

A non-technical evaluation

Phone screenings are a great opportunity to look at factors that don't necessarily have to do with engineering at all: a candidate's personality, politics, and past experience. The first is simple; the interview as a whole will give you an idea of whether the candidate has a good attitude and is easy to communicate with.

Give your interviewees' resumes a careful read before the interview, and be sure to ask clarifying questions about a candidate's accomplishments during the interview. Asking a candidate to tell you about him or herself during the first part of the interview is a great strategy; as they walk you through their career history, ask specifically about what they wrote on their resume to guide the conversation. Good candidates will have a consistent story about their experience and will add relevant details.

Look for instances on candidates' resumes where they faced a challenge in an interpersonal or political sense: businesses or projects they founded, teams they led, new technologies they championed the adoption of. Ask questions that will help you get a sense of the people involved in these challenges and how the candidate related to them. Have a look at the following examples:

> Poor question:

  "Tell me about a time when you had to take leadership of a project."

  These questions are hard to answer and you probably won't get much insight.

> Better question:

  "Your resume says you led a three person team at Company X. Tell me about how you came to be in charge and how you managed your team's work."

  You can continue asking clarifying questions about this situation until you really understand how the candidate handled him or herself.

Technical evaluation

At least a third of your phone screening time should be devoted to technical questions or challenges. If your engineering team is on the small side, consider holding technical phone screenings with two or three engineering team members. Although this compounds the man hours necessary for a phone screening, it can be very useful. Your employees can ask candidates how they would handle a challenge that the employee has personally run into.

Even if your expertise has nothing to do with engineering, you can certainly expect to get an accurate picture of how technically skilled a candidate is. One type of question I favor is the "explain it like I'm five" variety—ask the candidate to explain a technical concept to you while assuming that you have no background knowledge of technology at all. Listen carefully and ask the candidate to clarify any technical terms they use or assumptions they make. Good candidates will leave you with a clear understanding of even very abstract or specialized concepts.

Tip

Don't make interviewees write code during phone screenings. It's a waste of valuable time, as both of you sit in silence while the candidate scrambles to write something that works, then spends minutes awkwardly reciting every semicolon and parenthesis back to you. Code tests or pair programming during in-person interviews are much better ways to evaluate coding ability.

Avoid trick questions and puzzles in phone screenings. Remember that this is meant to be a quick, early-stage evaluation where the candidate is learning as much about your company as you are about them. Keep the conversation moving, and if you want to see how candidates handle a challenge, ask them how they'd solve real-world problems or design a particular system.

An example of a technical challenge would be as follows: "Our graphic designer wants to review all of the icons in our codebase to make sure that they are consistent. Knowing that our codebase consists of many gigabytes and tens of thousands of files in a nested directory structure, how would you go about finding all of the image files?"

The first answer to this question is simple; a good candidate should be able to pick from any number of technologies and describe a simple script which loops through all of the files in the directory and makes a list of all the files that match image file extensions. From here, you can add additional constraints to the problem to see how the candidate handles them. How would they make this list of icons available as a web-based tool? How would they go about allowing the graphic designer to search the list? You can continue in this way until you are confident that the candidate knows enough to think on their feet about solving problems and can explain their solutions in sufficient detail.

Be wary of candidates who only know one technology, tool, or programming language. If a candidate is steering every question back to a single technology they know very well, steer the conversation in a different direction by asking them about their understanding of more basic concepts (for example, Object Oriented Programming, Inheritance, system design, computer architecture, or logic). Or, if the position requires them to know other technologies, ask them how they would accomplish a goal explicitly using a different technology.

Wrapping up

You should always leave five or ten minutes at the end of a phone screening for the interviewee to ask you questions. Good candidates will be prepared with questions about your company and will want to fill in any gaps in their understanding of the role.

If a candidate has absolutely no questions for you, that can be a red flag. Most should have done at least a few minutes research on your company and what you do; the questions interviewees ask are a good way to judge their preparedness and enthusiasm about the position.

Expect to be asked about all aspects of your business, not just engineering. Good candidates will be interested in your business model, customers, office life, company history, and leadership. Questions about remuneration, benefits, and perks are less appropriate at this stage, but interviewees may clarify information you put in your job description.

After that, finishing up the phone screening is as simple as thanking the interviewee for their time and informing them of when they can expect to hear from you again.

Summary

In this chapter, we learned:

> ➤ What your goals should be during a phone screening
> ➤ How to evaluate a candidate's personality, politics, and past experience
> ➤ The best kinds of technical questions to ask
> ➤ Red flags to look out for with respect to a candidate's technical knowledge
> ➤ How to evaluate candidates based on the questions they ask you

The next chapter will teach you how to use code tests or technical projects as another screening tool for candidates.

> 4

Code Tests

One fairly specialized and increasingly common method of evaluating candidates is a code test. The employer decides on a small technical problem that a qualified candidate should be able to solve, and requires candidates to solve it before moving forward. These tests are interesting because the candidate works through them in their own time and submits the results to the employer.

This type of candidate evaluation is usually only used for software engineering or other programming-focused jobs, so this chapter will be applicable mostly to hiring for these types of positions. However, even if you're hiring for an engineer who won't do much programming, it might be useful to consider what administering these kinds of pre-interview evaluations might tell you.

In this chapter, you will learn:

> How to write a good test that will tell you how qualified a candidate is

> When in the hiring process to implement a code test

> How to evaluate candidates' solutions to tests

Writing tests

What kind of technical problem makes a good code test? In general, a problem should:

➤ Reflect a real-world task that you would expect an engineer to be able to solve on their first day of work with no knowledge of your engineering infrastructure

➤ Not require specialized tools or resources, possibly other than data you will provide the candidate

➤ Take two to four hours to complete

The first point is by far the most important. You will get a much better idea of a candidate's ability to do the job if you give them a test that looks like a task they would work on if they were hired tomorrow. The candidate will benefit from a clearer understanding of the type of work you will expect them to do as well.

An example test would be as follows: "Using only HTML, CSS, and Javascript, create a single web page that consumes an RSS feed and presents it as an attractive list of well-formatted feed entries, including item metadata. When the user clicks on a particular feed entry in the list, they should be presented with a "detailed view" for that entry including more complete metadata."

This is a test for a more junior frontend engineer position. It is technically fairly simple, with the expectation that a basic solution can be put together in an hour or so. It does leave room for creativity, and better candidates will be able to present more attractive and well-organized solutions. This is a particularly good test in that the position deals extensively with consuming data from external APIs and feeds. Thus the test is well suited for the level of the position and the type of work it involves.

Clearly communicating exactly what you wish the candidate to accomplish is very important. Be clear about what kind of input a piece of code should accept and what kind of output it should produce. Be sure to specify what deliverables you expect, and be prepared to assist candidates with any questions they may have.

Administering tests

Administering a code test is as simple as sending candidates an e-mail with the instructions and any necessary additional resources they will need. Be clear about the time frame in which you expect an answer; a week is usually plenty of time.

Code tests can be administered at a variety of points during the hiring process, and determining when that is depends on what's convenient for your company and what makes sense for the individual position. In general, for lower-level positions where you'll receive more resumes, it makes sense to administer code tests earlier in the process as a quick way to narrow the field. If you have fewer interviewing resources, it also makes sense to do code tests before the phone screening.

Make a note

You may also choose to administer a "live" code test during a phone screening if you want to watch candidates work in real time using a collaborative editing tool such as Google Docs. Live tests can cut down the evaluation time per candidate, but they are generally more suited to shorter coding tasks that will take an hour or so to solve. Try incorporating live code exercises into your phone screenings and see what works for you.

Your experience may vary, however; you may find that you get more code test responses (and better ones) after doing a preliminary phone screening with a candidate. Feel free to experiment with the order and track what is more successful for you.

Grading tests

Narrowing the pool to a few good candidates and asking them to complete a more complex, realistic task tells you more than administering an easy test to lots of candidates.

Complex tests take more time to grade, however. I recommend having a few engineers review the code, noting where they would have done things differently. Keeping the anonymized test code around for future reference may be useful if you're using the same test on many engineers.

Generally, writing code that works is the most important metric to look at when grading. However, you should also pay attention to:

> How well organized and readable the code is. Evaluating code this way will come naturally to your engineers; they should be able to easily follow the candidate's reasoning. Code should be organized into logical units (methods, functions, classes, objects, and so on). The candidate should additionally follow good naming conventions and avoid repeating code.

> How well the candidate tests for edge cases and error conditions. Good candidates will handle invalid or unexpected inputs to their code and output clear error messages.

Summary

In this chapter, we learned how to:

> Write tests that reflect the actual problems your engineers solve

> Decide when is best to administer a test for a given position

> Grade tests based on both performance and organization

If you've come this far, you've narrowed the field of candidates to just a few top contenders. The next chapter will cover possibly the most important evaluation of all: the in-person interview.

> 5

In-person Interviews

The in-person interview is the most important and the most resource-intensive step in the hiring process. For the interview organizer, it is a challenge both to schedule candidates and to prepare interviewers to make the best possible decision. Interviewers must prepare their questions and criteria for hiring in advance, as well as prepare to be a good ambassador for their company. And of course, candidates must be ready for nearly a full day's mental challenge!

If you've screened your candidates well, you've given the candidates who come in to meet your team the best possible chance at success. This chapter will ensure that your whole team is prepared to make the ultimate decision on which candidate to hire.

This chapter will teach you how to:

> ➤ Manage interview scheduling and logistics
> ➤ Train technical interviewers
> ➤ Structure an individual interview
> ➤ Ask good technical interview questions

Organizing the interview

The modern engineering interview is a long and complex affair, often lasting a full day. It is important that interviewees be evaluated both by their prospective peers as well as management. As the interview coordinator, you will be responsible for scheduling the interviewee to come in, recruiting interviewers, and determining the order of the day's schedule, organizing food and drink as necessary, and making sure that resources such as conference rooms are free for interview use.

Having a clear and predetermined framework for interview days will help the process of organization go smoothly. A standard engineering interview is a four to six hour day during which a candidate meets around five individual interviewers for no more than one hour each. Generally these interviewers will include at least one manager and engineers who are at or above the candidate's skill level. It's best to schedule at least one break during interviews more than four hours long; usually a group of your team members will schedule lunch with the interviewee. This isn't compulsory, but it's a nice opportunity to get an idea of how the interviewee fits in with the team.

I strongly suggest that you develop a comprehensive interview guide for your interviewees. This should be a document where you lay out the schedule for the day (when to arrive, when to expect to leave, any meals you will be providing), how to get to your office (including how to navigate various street entrances, elevators, security, and who to ask for when the candidate arrives at your office), anything the interviewee should bring with them, and any other guidelines you may have. Putting the general structure of the day in writing will set interviewees at ease and drastically reduce the volume of questions you'll have to answer.

You should of course adjust the general interview framework to what works for your company and your team. Involve your team members early in the process to make sure everyone understands their role. Keeping the process of scheduling as transparent as possible will help interview days go smoothly.

Training interviewers

Selecting which of your engineers will interview a candidate is an important task. You want to choose team members who are not too senior or junior in experience to the interview candidate, as they will be better prepared to evaluate that candidate's skill level in relation to their own. Interviewers who communicate well, are able put candidates at ease, and can answer questions easily should be on your shortlist as well. Remember that you want to put the best face of your company forward, and that the employees who meet a candidate will be ambassadors for your company.

You should always be expanding your pool of potential interviewers to make scheduling easier. Having less experienced interviewers shadow your more seasoned employees for a few interviews will be immensely helpful in getting them up to speed.

Always make sure that your interviewers know the schedule for the day and have the candidate's resume well in advance—make sure you send timely reminders to interviewers to ensure their attendance. It would not be good to leave an interviewee alone in a conference room because an interviewer forgot to show up, or to have flustered and unprepared interviewers making candidates feel unwelcome.

Your goal is to help new interviewers be organized and prepared in advance for their task. A sample outline like the one in the next section may be very helpful; some companies even build up databases of interview questions that their interviewers can use.

One-hour interview outline

If you are going to be one of the interviewers for an engineering candidate, it's best to have a solid plan in advance for your interview. You can use this general outline and customize it for the questions you want to ask and your goals for the interview. Encourage your colleagues to use a similar outline or provide one when training interviewers.

It's common among engineers to say that the only real criteria for hiring someone is that they're "smart and get things done." Does a candidate really understand the difficult technical concepts involved in engineering and do they have the critical thinking skills necessary to solve difficult problems? Do they take initiative in accomplishing goals? If it helps you to think of the interviewee in terms of "smart and gets things done", definitely use that criteria to help frame your questions and your ultimate evaluation of potential hires.

Introduction

Tell the candidate a little about yourself and what you do. A few minutes of small talk helps to put everyone at ease and makes the candidate feel less stressed. Set the stage for your interview; let the candidate know whether they'll be writing code on a whiteboard, for example. If you're the first interviewer of the day, briefly reiterate what will be coming next for the interviewee, so everyone is on the same page.

Ask about the candidate's experience

You can ask general questions about recent projects or get more specific about how candidates have solved problems relevant to your business. You're looking for candidates who get passionate about what they work on. Always ask follow-up questions about how the interviewee took the lead in solving problems and accomplishing goals.

An easy technical question

This is a warm up for the candidate to switch over to technical problem-solving mode. It's also a quick red flag for you if the interviewee struggles with it. We'll see some examples of simple technical warm-ups in the next section.

An in-depth technical question

This should be a fairly complex challenge. Think of it as an opportunity to see how the candidate thinks through a problem as you give them hints and shape their understanding. We'll discuss how to format more in-depth technical questions in the next section as well.

Sell your company

Transition away from the mental stress of technical questions by telling the candidate why your company is a great place to work. What recent projects have you personally been excited about? What challenges could the candidate look forward to helping your team solve?

Interviewee questions and wrap-up

Give the candidate an opportunity to ask you questions. They're likely to have had other interviewers before you, so don't penalize a candidate for not coming up with a new question for every interviewer. Thank the candidate for their time and hand them off to the next interviewer or see them to their next activity of the day.

Make your recommendation

As a general rule, you should be making your decision while the interview is still fresh in your mind. I would recommend against talking to the other interviewers before you do this, to avoid biasing your opinion. Your focus during the interview is to remove a candidate from the "maybe" pile in your head to a definite hire or no-hire. If you're still ambivalent after the interview, it's generally a sign that you should recommend against hiring this person. Even if you are not the final decision maker, you should be forming a list of each candidate's strengths and potential risks to present to the hiring manager.

No matter the outline you choose to use for your interviews, having a detailed plan will help you stick to a schedule and properly evaluate candidates. Feeling rushed or realizing you skipped important interview sections is never a good feeling, so I encourage that you plan your interview structure and questions in advance.

Technical interview questions

Generally, if you're asking technical questions to an interviewing candidate, you need to be in a position to really understand what a competent solution looks like. You must also be able to ask probing questions to a candidate to really understand their thought processes, and to give them hints when they get stuck. Whether you're a technical manager or engineer, or just advising new interviewers, this section will advise you on how to format your technical questions.

Quick and easy questions

No matter the type of engineer you're interviewing, it's good to have an easy warm-up question. Have a mechanical engineer sketch a simple free-body diagram and solve a given problem. Have a programmer write a function to calculate the circumference of a circle given the radius. You're not necessarily looking for whether the candidate can solve the problem or not; ideally, everyone you bring in will be good enough to solve a very simple question. You're looking for the speed, ease, and confidence with which a really great candidate will solve it.

"Find the bug" questions can be both quick and useful if you ask them correctly. Present the candidate with a piece of code, system diagram, circuit, and so on, which has both major and minor issues: components connected backwards, syntax errors, or fundamental issues in design or performance. See which problems a candidate picks up on and ask them what their correct solution would look like.

In-depth technical questions

Once you've gotten an interviewee over the hurdle of a simple question or two and are confident in their skills, you should have at least one longer, challenging question in mind that you can discuss with the candidate for 10 to 15 minutes or so.

Technical challenges should vary broadly, but most fall into either design/architecture challenges or algorithm questions. The first type requires the candidate to design a fairly large, complex system at a high level. For instance, in a software engineering interview, this should not require writing code, but rather diagramming complex client-server interactions or the relationships between different types of objects. The second question actually requires a candidate to present a working solution to a somewhat smaller problem.

Some of the best challenge questions will come from the actual work your engineers do every day. Start with a very broad problem statement that mirrors something you built recently: "Talk me through how you would build a product/feature that accomplishes X goal." Ask the candidate about what tools they would use. Challenge the assumptions they make about how the end product should work. As they talk, add new constraints to the problem to see how they deal with increasing complexity or unexpected technical issues.

If you are asking a candidate to write code or draw precise diagrams, don't worry too much about asking a question that is overly difficult as long as you are willing to provide hints along the way. If a candidate finishes their solution, ask them to go back and find bugs, analyze the speed and performance of their code, or find ways to optimize their solution. Pay attention to how candidates react when you point out flaws in their solutions as well, as this may reveal important personality traits that may or may not suit your team.

What not to ask

There are some certain types of questions to avoid. Most of these are all too common in engineering interviews, but more people are coming to realize that they don't really tell you anything about a candidate's intelligence or ability to do the job.

Trivia questions

> *"Why is a manhole cover round?"*

Quizzing a candidate on what facts they remember or about the minutiae of the tools of engineering is almost never a good idea.

Estimation or "impossible" questions

> *"How many gas stations are there in San Francisco?"*

The theory is that the answers to this question don't matter; they're more about asking the candidate to think through the problem and seeing how they structure an answer. The problem is that this question has absolutely nothing to do with engineering. You can better see how an engineer thinks through a problem by asking them open-ended engineering questions that are much more like problems they would solve in the real world.

Brain teasers and logic puzzles

> *"You have three light switches, only one of which controls a light bulb inside a sealed box. If you can only open the box once, how do you figure out which switch controls the light bulb?"*

Brain teasers mainly rely on the candidate already knowing the answer or sitting in silence until the solution suddenly dawns on them. Neither are very good for evaluating a candidate's skills as an engineer.

Summary

In this chapter, you learned how to:

> ➤ Organize an interview schedule in a transparent and efficient way
> ➤ Recruit the best possible employees to be interviewers
> ➤ Create an interview plan to keep yourself organized
> ➤ Ask the right technical questions

The end of the interview process is not quite the end of the hiring funnel. As we wrap up, we will cover the last few important steps for following up after an interview and making a hiring decision.

> 6

Follow-up, Negotiation, and Closing a Hire

Due to the expense and manpower necessary to interview technical talent, it is incredibly important to organize all of the communication that needs to happen after a candidate is interviewed.

You may be in charge of collecting hiring feedback from the interviewing team, which should be done in a timely and efficient manner. You may also find yourself in the position of communicating with candidates, either making offers of employment or politely informing them that they will not be moving forward in the hiring process.

Whatever your role, this is the final step toward your ultimate goal of convincing a great engineer to join your team.

This chapter will teach you how to:

> Manage the hiring decision-making process

> Follow up with candidates after an interview

> Make your employment offers attractive to new employees

> Get your new employees started on the right foot

Making hiring decisions

The actual hiring decision involves a lot of people: team members, managers, HR representatives, and even executives. It's important to be organized to expedite communication between all of these parties.

As mentioned in the previous chapter, individual interviewers should be making their hire or no-hire recommendations as quickly as possible after they actually interview a candidate. Get individual feedback from interviewers before they discuss it with each other to preserve their unbiased impressions. Encourage interviewers to give written feedback, especially if you know it's going to take a few days (or weeks) to actually get the hiring approval.

When you have the interview feedback in hand, the final decision-making process will vary from company to company. You may find yourself in the position of translating all of the interview feedback into a definite hire or no-hire decision. Negative feedback from interviewers is inevitable; decide what your threshold is for considering a candidate as a definite no-hire. Generally, if more than two interviewers recommend against hiring, it's worth a very serious look at why they did so, if not outrightly rejecting the candidate.

The decision is not always crystal clear, however. At this stage in the process, you have a few more resources at your disposal to help you make your decision.

Checking references

Definitely check the engineer's references. Good candidates will provide them to you on request; generally they're not included in resumes. You should be looking to talk to a combination of former managers as well as teammates in order to get a complete picture of a candidate.

Ask about the candidate's technical accomplishments as well as their interactions with their team. If you have specific concerns about a candidate, now is your opportunity to ask someone with firsthand experience.

You may consider asking the referees whether there's anyone else at their company who worked closely with the candidate whom you should talk to. "Back-channel" references take a little more work to follow through with, but may get you a more complete picture of what a candidate is actually like.

Red flags

The following red flags are all very serious indicators that you shouldn't hire a candidate.

Personality conflict with a team member

If any of your team members find a candidate irritating, arrogant, or offensive after an interview, you run the very real risk of negatively impacting your team dynamic by hiring that person.

Conflicting stories

If what a candidate tells you in an interview conflicts greatly with what's on their resume or what their references tell you, I would strongly advise against hiring that person. Anything from an unexplained discrepancy to outright deception is a red flag.

Bad-mouthing former employers

Candidates should have good reasons why they left former positions or are looking for a career change. If they are strongly bitter or antagonistic toward former employers, this may reflect poor decision making skills or combative personality issues that you don't want on your team.

Communicating with candidates

A post-interview follow up is important to candidates. They took the time to come in and interview, so will look favorably on your company if you follow up to tell them what they should expect next.

At the end of the interview, have an exit conversation with each candidate thanking them for their time and giving them some idea of when they should expect to hear back from you with a decision. If you give candidates a definite answer on this (for example, "by the end of the week"), either be sure to actually follow through in that time frame or send a follow-up email to let them know about significant delays.

Make a note

Why spend the time and energy following up? Every candidate has experienced the company who tells them that they'll hear back within a certain number of days and then never calls, or the company who goes completely silent after the interview and calls back months later with an offer. You may have very real organizational issues that cause this kind of behavior that you can't personally solve. However, this kind of communication breakdown makes your company look bad and may cause you to lose candidates you put a lot of time into interviewing.

Letters of rejection

Having to write rejection letters is inevitable during such a long and selective process. It's tough news to get, but a polite phone call or e-mail telling a candidate they won't be moving forward is much better than simply never hearing back from a company.

Do expect candidates to ask you for feedback on what they could have done differently. This may not be feasible; you don't want to start an argument with a candidate over why they weren't hired. If you like, you might include a fairly general note in your letter of rejection, saying something like:

> *"We didn't feel that your skills and experience were a match for this position at this time. Keep honing your skills, and if you see any positions with our company that interest you in the future, we welcome your application."*

Sometimes you will encounter great engineers that, for one reason or another, you simply can't hire. It's entirely possible that your first-choice candidate may not work out, or that you may want to bring a candidate back in for a different position in the future. Be as honest as you can with these valuable candidates and ask their permission to contact them in the future. Maintaining a great impression and relationship with them now may turn into an easy hire in the future.

Employment offers and compensation

So you've found a great engineer and have approval to hire them; wonderful! The employment offer is the last chance you have to market your company to an engineering hire. Outside of the standard negotiations for salary and stock options, what can you offer engineers to make working for your company more valuable and attractive?

Conferences and education expenses

Engineers should always be honing their skills and learning new tools. By offering to send your employees to a certain number of conferences per year or cover education expenses, you build a more valuable employee and tell prospective hires that you value their personal growth.

Relocation expenses

With the scarcity of top talent, it's often necessary to hire engineers who will need to relocate for work. Make it clear that your company will cover their expenses and make the transition process as smooth as possible.

Health and wellness benefits

Covering gym memberships, meals, or other benefits that will keep your employees happy and healthy will make it clear that you care about more than an engineer's technical work output.

Flexible hours

While you may want your employees to benefit from being in the same place as their team, it's important to consider whether you may realize more employee happiness by allowing them to set their own schedules or work remotely for a certain amount of time. This may be more of a personal consideration than an across-the-board policy; new parents or prospective hires who will have to commute may particularly appreciate the offer to let them work from home on certain days.

The personal touch

Sometimes it's not material benefits that convince a prospective hire to join your team. Feeling that they are joining a great team with a great manager can sometimes make all the difference. Give new hires room to reach out to their new team members and managers and ask them any questions they may have. Making offers over the phone or in person is also useful as candidates can immediately get answers to questions or concerns. Anything that speeds up the often time-sensitive offer negotiation process is beneficial.

On boarding new hires

Engineers as a group generally want to spend as little time on the logistics of starting a new job as they can, and want to start contributing to your team as quickly as possible. What can you do to support them?

If you're relocating a new hire, there's a lot you can do in helping them adapt to their new home. Beyond just covering expenses and moving, you might provide small personal touches like guides to great local restaurants, entertainment, and amenities. Organizing a social event or outing for your new hire and their teammates is beneficial for everyone on the team and an appropriate welcome for your new employee.

Engineers generally have a clear idea of what equipment they're going to need on day one. Communicate with new hires and make sure they have all the computing hardware and software they need in addition to whatever essentials your current team calls for. It should go without saying that an engineer's desk should be set up and ready when they walk in the door!

Assign new engineers a team member mentor. This should be someone who will be working with the new hire in the long term and can answer any questions about your company's engineering infrastructure and tools.

Summary

In this chapter, we wrapped up the hiring process by learning how to:

> ➤ Collect interview feedback to make an informed hiring decision
>
> ➤ Follow up with candidates about whether or not they got the job
>
> ➤ Tailor your compensation packages to make engineers happy
>
> ➤ Prepare for a new engineering hire's first day of work

We've now wrapped up our step-by-step guide to the process of finding, interviewing, and hiring engineering talent. With the practical tips, outlines, and examples provided here, you should be able to tailor your company's hiring practices to hire top engineers. You have learned to recruit and identify talented candidates early in the process. You have also learned how to accurately evaluate candidates through interviews and tests. Finally, you have learned how to increase your organization's confidence in making hiring decisions and convince engineers who are a great fit for your company to work for you!